The 2007
Commemorative
Stamp Yearbook

Other books available from the United States Postal Service:

The 2006 Commemorative Stamp Yearbook

The Postal Service Guide to U.S. Stamps—34th Edition

The 2007
Commemorative
Stamp Yearbook

UNITED STATES
POSTAL SERVICE.

Collins
An Imprint of HarperCollinsPublishers

2007 COMMEMORATIVE STAMP YEARBOOK.
Copyright © 2007 by the United States Postal Service. All rights reserved.
Printed in the United States of America. No part of this book may be
used or reproduced in any manner whatsoever without written
permission except in the case of brief quotations embodied in critical
articles and reviews. For information address HarperCollins Publishers,
10 East 53rd Street, New York, NY 10022.

The designs of stamps and postal stationery are the subject of individual
copyrights by the United States Postal Service. UNITED STATES
POSTAL SERVICE, the eagle logo, and POSTAL SERVICE
are trademarks of the United States Postal Service.

Star Wars © 2007 Lucasfilm Ltd. & TM. All rights reserved.
Used under authorization.
Ella Fitzgerald® licensed by CMG Worldwide, Indianapolis, IN.

HarperCollins books may be purchased for educational,
business, or sales promotional use. For information please write:
Special Markets Department, HarperCollins Publishers,
10 East 53rd Street, New York, NY 10022.

Library of Congress Cataloging-in-Publication Data
has been applied for.

ISBN: 978-0-06-123685-3
ISBN-10: 0-06-123685-3

07 08 09 10 11 ❖ 10 9 8 7 6 5 4 3 2 1

Contents

USA 41

Aurora Borealis

1607
THE SETTL

Contents

James Stewart

USA 41

2007 41

USA

MENT OF JAMESTOWN

41
USA

2007

UMPQUA RIVER, OREGON

They come forth from the darkness, and their sails
Gleam for a moment only in the blaze,
And eager faces, as the light unveils
Gaze at the tower, and vanish while they gaze.

So wrote Henry Wadsworth Longfellow in his poem "The Lighthouse," an ode to the sentinels that literally and symbolically "bring man nearer unto man." This year, as the commemorative program highlights the 200th anniversary of Longfellow's birth, the U.S. Postal Service also unveils a new set of lighthouses stamps, all part of its annual effort to honor an array of worthy subjects that help bring us together as a nation.

From the glasswork of Louis Comfort Tiffany to the beguiling mysteries of the polar lights, this year's stamps reflect the natural and man-made wonders around us. With vivid artwork sure to entice collectors and the mailing public alike, the 2007 collection transports us to the arctic tundra—and puts us behind the wheels of vintage speedboats.

Lively portraits capture the essence of memorable entertainers such as James Stewart and Ella Fitzgerald, while magical characters highlight the art of Disney, and an eye-popping *Star Wars* sheet takes us to fantastic worlds.

The stamps in this book commemorate inspiring aspects of American civic life as well. One new stamp reaffirms the importance of jury service, while another spotlights a key school-desegregation decision. Meanwhile, a special commemorative honors Gerald R. Ford with a portrait that recalls the dignity of our 38th president.

Each year, the Commemorative Stamp Yearbook celebrates the best America has to offer. These miniature masterpieces become part of the historical record, and many of them may indeed prove timeless, just like Longfellow's lighthouse:

Year after year, through all the silent night
Burns on forevermore that quenchless flame,
Shines on that inextinguishable light!

Ella Fitzgerald®

It was obvious

how much Ella Fitzgerald loved to sing. She communicated the joy it gave her in every note and spoke of it often. "The only thing better than singing," she remarked, "is more singing."

When art director Ethel Kessler took the Ella Fitzgerald assignment for 2007, she knew she wanted a stamp that caught something of Ella's style—not a traditional, "serious" portrait but something that captured her sense of humor, her sense of the dramatic. "We first looked at using a photograph of Ella in a jazz club," Kessler explains. "It was moody and full of smoke, but Ella was lost in all of the nightclub atmosphere. I asked Paul Davis to work with me on a portrait because I knew that a Davis painting could bring out her sparkle."

Fitzgerald had a lot of sparkle; as a girl, she made her friends laugh by telling them she was going to be famous. By the time she was 16, Fitzgerald was dancing on the streets of New York for tips. In 1934, she entered an amateur talent show at the famed Apollo Theater, planning to dance. At the last minute, she decided to sing instead—and won the competition. A short time later she sang in another talent competition at the Harlem Opera Show and was declared the winner there, too. Bandleader and drummer Chick Webb soon hired her to sing with his orchestra. In 1938, they had a number one hit record with "A-Tisket, A-Tasket," a novelty song Fitzgerald co-wrote with Van Alexander; she was barely more than 20 years old, and she had made good on her childhood boast. "It isn't where you came from," she would say later, "it's where you're going that counts."

Fitzgerald was heading straight for the center of American musical life. After demonstrating her mastery of swing music, she developed an interest in bebop—a new musical style that she explored while sitting in with trumpeter Dizzy Gillespie and his band during jam sessions. Gillespie, an inventor of the new style, encouraged Fitzgerald to experiment. "Listening to Dizzy made me want to try something with my voice that would be like a horn," Fitzgerald said. "He'd shout 'Go ahead and blow' and I'd improvise." Her 1945 recording of the song "Flying Home," showcasing her interest in bebop, is considered a masterpiece of scat singing—the vocalizing of nonsense syllables, as if the singer were an instrumental soloist.

FACING PAGE: Ella at the Downbeat Club in New York City, 1949.

In the 1950s, Fitzgerald began work on her landmark series of "Songbook" recordings. This historic series presented memorable versions of more than 200 American standards by composers such as Harold Arlen, Irving Berlin, Duke Ellington, and the Gershwins, among others. In addition, Fitzgerald collaborated with other giants of jazz, including Louis Armstrong, Count Basie, and Oscar Peterson. Throughout her life, she toured extensively, becoming one of the first black artists to appear in various exclusive clubs. In 1961, she sang at the inaugural gala for President John F. Kennedy. She continued to tour long past the time when other singers retire. "I get a little tired sometimes," she once said, "but whenever I get on a stage and the public is there, I forget all the tiredness."

In addition to her stage performances, Fitzgerald also appeared in a few Hollywood films, including the Abbott and Costello comedy *Ride 'Em Cowboy* (1942), *St. Louis Blues* (1958), and *Let No Man Write My Epitaph* (1960). She played a singer in *Pete Kelly's Blues* (1955), giving us a glimpse of what it might have been like to see her perform live at a nightclub.

A nightclub setting was chosen for the stamp art, in which Fitzgerald shimmers in front of an orange spotlight against a dark background. Paul Davis's portrait does indeed capture the joy and vibrancy of his subject. "I sing like I feel," Fitzgerald once said, and the stamp art encapsulates the depth of that feeling while honoring her lifetime of achievement.

"The only thing better than singing is more singing."

LEFT: Ira Gershwin once commented, "I never knew how good our songs were until I heard Ella Fitzgerald sing them."
RIGHT: Ella records "Back on the Block" with Quincy Jones in 1989.

Oklahoma Statehood

In the early 1900s, two separate entities came together to form a new state: the Indian Territory, which included members of more than 60 indigenous and relocated Native American groups, and the Oklahoma Territory, home to numerous non-Indian settlers. Delegates from both territories wrote a constitution for the proposed state, and voters in both territories approved the document, paving the way for federal recognition. On November 16, 1907, Oklahoma became the 46th state in the Union.

Today, Oklahoma is home to about 3.5 million people, including more than 350,000 Native Americans. Stamp artist Mike Larsen prides himself on his connections to Oklahoma history. A member of the Chickasaw Nation, Larsen has painted portraits of the tribe's Living Elders. He was also commissioned to create several murals for the State Capitol Rotunda and the Oklahoma Art Institute.

For the stamp subject, Larsen chose sunrise on the Cimarron River, which has played an important role in Oklahoma history. From 1821 until 1880, the southern branch of the Santa Fe Trail ran along its banks; millions of cattle crossed it on the way north from Texas to Kansas along the Chisholm Trail. In 1889, would-be settlers poured across the river in the first of several government sponsored land runs.

The nickname "Sooner State" derives from these early land runs, when white settlers entered and staked claims to lands "sooner" than the officially designated time. In 1908, more than a decade after the last land run, the word began to take on a new meaning when the University of Oklahoma named its football team the Oklahoma Sooners. As the team grew more popular, so did the nickname, and before long many residents of the 46th state were calling themselves Sooners, too.

Today, Oklahoma has a thriving economy based largely on agriculture, service industries, and oil and gas. It also has one of the busiest river ports in the United States: the Tulsa Port of Catoosa, which sits at the head of the McClellan-Kerr Arkansas River Navigation System, a 445-mile waterway linking the state with ports on the Mississippi River and beyond. Oklahomans continue to excel in many other fields as well, including education, business and finance, science and medicine, and aviation and aerospace.

LEFT: Oklahoma City as viewed from the Bricktown district. FACING PAGE: The elegant dome on the Oklahoma State Capitol was completed in 2002.

With Love and Kisses

Since 1973, the U.S. Postal Service has offered philatelic variations on the timeless theme of love. The first Love stamp, a colorful eight-cent issuance featuring a design by pop artist Robert Indiana, proved so popular that more than 300 million were printed. Since then, subsequent Love stamps have featured a delightful assortment of designs, including heart motifs, eye-popping flowers, traditional cherubs, and colorful abstractions.

Two candy hearts decorated the 2004 Love stamp, but this year marks the debut of the sweetest of treats: chocolate. Evoking images of sweet and ardent affection, this new Love stamp features a silver Hershey's Kisses chocolate on a deep red background. The shape of the Kisses chocolate mirrors the form of the passionate red heart that rises behind it.

The unmistakable shape of Hershey's Kisses chocolates has not changed since The Hershey Company introduced this milk-chocolate candy to the nation in 1907. Wrapped by hand until the process was automated in 1921, Kisses chocolates have been available year round for 100 years, with only one exception: production ceased from 1942 to 1949, when silver foil was rationed during the war effort. Kisses chocolates wrapped in red and silver foil were introduced in 1986 in honor of Valentine's Day.

The artwork for this new stamp was created by José Ortega, the award-winning illustrator who previously designed the Salsa stamp, one of four that appeared as part of the 2005 Let's Dance–Bailemos issuance. Utilizing his flair for movement and bright color, Ortega has created a passionate and playful design—encouragement to seal all our letters with a kiss.

HERSHEY'S

REG. U.S. PAT OFF.

Henry Wadsworth Longfellow

Listen, my children, and you shall hear

Of the midnight ride of Paul Revere,

On the eighteenth of April, in Seventy-five;

Hardly a man is now alive

Who remembers that famous day and year.

"Each had his tale to tell, and each / Was anxious to be pleased and please," wrote Henry Wadsworth Longfellow (1807–1882) in the prelude to *Tales of a Wayside Inn*, his delightful collection of narrative poems drawn from European and American sources. More than a century later, perusing the collected works of Longfellow can be likened to sitting in a New England inn in days gone by and listening to the master storytellers of the age.

Often considered the "uncrowned poet laureate" of 19th-century America, Longfellow wrote more than 400 poems. Many of his shorter works, including "A Psalm of Life" and "Excelsior," were highly popular, and he was equally renowned for long narrative poems such as *The Courtship of Miles Standish* and *The Song of Hiawatha*. Longfellow was widely read during his lifetime and became a venerable figure not only in the United States, where he was invited to dine with presidents, but also internationally.

As a professor of modern languages at Harvard and a skilled translator, Longfellow imitated and adapted European forms, from the Middle English of Geoffrey Chaucer to the epic poetry of Finland, while adding immeasurably to the American literary vernacular. When we speak of "ships that pass in the night," we quote from Longfellow's "The Theologian's Tale." When a nature documentary begins with the stirring words "This is the forest primeval," it invokes the first line of *Evangeline*.

Issued on the 200th anniversary of Longfellow's birth, this 23rd stamp in the Literary Arts series evokes the opening of "Paul Revere's Ride," his most famous poem. With these famous lines, Longfellow reminds us why his contemporaries found his poetry so compelling—and why subsequent generations have heeded his exhortation to *listen*.

BACKGROUND: Grant Wood's 1931 painting *The Midnight Ride of Paul Revere*. ABOVE: A dashing young Longfellow painted by Cephas Giovanni Thompson in 1840.

Settlement of Jamestown

Under the command of Captain Christopher Newport, three ships—*Susan Constant*, *Godspeed*, and *Discovery*—left docks near London on December 20, 1606. Charged with establishing a colony in the New World, the expedition arrived in Virginia on April 26, 1607. England had failed in previous attempts to build lasting settlements in the Americas, most notably on Roanoke Island in the 1580s, but expectations were high that this new effort would succeed.

On May 13, 1607, expedition leaders selected a site more than 30 miles up the James River from the Chesapeake Bay. The location, a marshy peninsula that became an island at high tide, offered good moorings. Connected to the mainland by a narrow strip of land, the site seemed easily defended. It was also far enough upriver, the men hoped, to escape the notice of Spanish warships patrolling the Atlantic coast.

On May 14, all of the men went ashore, cleared a patch of ground, and set up tents behind a simple brushwood fence, which quickly proved inadequate when

ABOVE: Captain John Smith, a leader of the Jamestown colony.
BACKGROUND: An engraving of early colonists.

JAMESTOWN

In 1607, colonists aboard the *Susan Constant*, *Godspeed*, and *Discovery* arrived in Virginia and founded Jamestown, the first permanent English settlement in the Americas. The painting below shows how the fortified town may have appeared during its early years.

1607 USA
THE SETTLEMENT OF JAMESTOWN

the colonists were set upon by Indians. The men soon built a more substantive structure. They also planted their first grain crop and began replacing their tents with small houses.

In the early days of the settlement, the weather was fair, the countryside lovely, and the hunting excellent. But as the seasons changed and relations with the Powhatan Indians worsened, conditions deteriorated, and disease, famine, polluted river water, and Indian attacks all took a terrible toll. By January 1608, fewer than forty were left to meet the next wave of settlers. Through the efforts of leaders such as Captain John Smith and entrepreneurs like John Rolfe, and with timely help from some of the local Indians—including Pocahontas, daughter of the chief of the Powhatan empire—Jamestown endured.

The town grew beyond the confines of the fort, and more settlements were established in the region. Jamestown became the first capital of Virginia, and on July 30, 1619, the first legislative assembly in English-speaking America was convened there.

Over the years, the fort at Jamestown was lost to history, but in 1994, archaeologists with the Association for the Preservation of Virginia Antiquities set out to find it. By late 1996, they had uncovered enough evidence, including traces of two walls, to prove they had located it. As part of the Jamestown Rediscovery Project, archaeologists continue to unearth artifacts that may tell us more about the lives of the people who founded and maintained the first permanent English settlement in the Americas.

This souvenir sheet commemorates that occasion with a stamp that features a 1949 painting by Griffith Baily Coale showing the original three ships under Captain Newport's command. The background is a painting by Richard Schlecht that appeared in the June 2002 issue of *National Geographic*; it has been updated for this sheet with the help of archaeologists. The revised art shows how the settlement may have looked during its earliest years, with "ghosted" areas representing sections that had not been excavated at the time of the update.

ABOVE: A modern reconstruction of the Jamestown settlement. RIGHT: The ship *Susan Constant* silhouetted on the James River. BACKGROUND: Richard Schlecht's painting was based on recent archaeological research.

STAR WARS™

Set across a fantastic galaxy of exotic planets and bizarre creatures, George Lucas's deceptively simple morality tale of good versus evil has resonated with generations of fans. On the 30th anniversary of the release of the original *Star Wars* film, this remarkable souvenir sheet recalls the sense of wonder that surrounds the most successful and popular epic adventure of all time.

In 1977, audiences thrilled to the story of Luke Skywalker, a moisture farmer on a desert planet who discovers that he is heir to a much larger destiny. While learning the ways of the Jedi Knights, a nearly extinct order of heroes whose abilities flow from a mystic power known as the Force, Luke plays a crucial role in the Rebellion against the sinister Darth Vader and the evil Galactic Empire. The first *Star Wars* film—now known as Episode IV *A New Hope*—won six Oscars, and Luke and his friends battled Vader in two sequels, *The Empire Strikes Back* and *Return of the Jedi*.

In 1999, fans again flocked to theaters to see the first new *Star Wars* film in 16 years. Episode I *The Phantom Menace* was the first in a trilogy of long-awaited prequels that depicted Darth Vader's dramatic rise to power. Set many years before the original movies, this new trilogy greatly expanded the *Star Wars* universe while attracting a new generation of young fans to the adventures of "A long time ago in a galaxy far, far away. . . . "

While becoming an integral and instantly recognizable part of American popular culture, the six movies in the *Star Wars* saga also brought numerous technical innovations to the art of film-

making. During the creation of the first film in 1977, George Lucas created his own visual effects company, Industrial Light & Magic, to handle more than 300 special-effects shots; today ILM is the recognized leader in digital effects. Lucasfilm's Skywalker Sound also set the standard for sound engineering and post-production video editing in the film and television industries. The 2002 release of *Star Wars*: Episode II *Attack of the Clones*, filmed entirely digitally, ensured that the *Star Wars* saga would remain the standard by which all other effects-oriented movies are judged.

This souvenir sheet features artwork by Drew Struzan, whose style is immediately recognizable not only from his portraits for recent stamps in the Legends of Hollywood series but also from his work on the evocative, collage-like *Star Wars* movie posters. Dominated by Darth Vader and featuring familiar characters and scenes, this sheet captures the dazzling visuals and sense of limitless adventure that have made *Star Wars* such a universal phenomenon.

Pollination

The transfer of pollen within flowers, or from one flower to another of the same species, is the basis for fruit and seed production. Insects and other animals, such as birds and bats, provide pollination services for the majority of the world's food crops and flowering plants. In turn, the plants provide their pollinators with food and other nutrients in the form of energy-producing nectar and protein-rich pollen. Some also serve as hosts for the larvae of insect pollinators.

Highly beneficial to humans, insect-pollinated plants alone provide us with about one-third of the foods we eat and the beverages we drink. In fact, some plant species—including red clover and other important farm crops—are pollinated only by bumblebees. Many fibers, condiments, spices, oils, and medicines also come from animal-pollinated plants. On a purely aesthetic level, we also enjoy the beautiful profusion of colors and lively fragrances that many flowers use to attract pollinators.

Unfortunately, some animal pollinators appear to be declining in numbers. As a result, many concerned organizations and individuals, along with some government agencies, are developing conservation and restoration projects while working to encourage pollinator research and awareness.

Many things can be done to help promote the health and vitality of pollinator populations: planting flower gardens that provide a continuous succession of blooms throughout the season; using nontoxic methods to control pests and weeds; protecting non-target organisms such as pollinators from inadvertent exposure to pesticides, insecticides, herbicides, and other chemicals; and setting aside and protecting habitats suitable for wild pollinators.

Featuring artwork by Steve Buchanan, these stamps illustrate the pollination partnership with a design that reinforces the interconnectedness of nature. In an interesting design twist, these four stamps are arranged in two alternating blocks that fit together like interlocking puzzles. In one block, the pollinators form a central starburst; in the other, the flowers are arranged in the center.

USA 41
USA 41
USA 41
USA 41
USA 41
USA 41
USA 41
USA 41

X11111

Pollination

Four different designs
Twenty 41¢ Self-adhesive Stamps
$8.20

© 2006 USPS

Bar Code
placed here

*H*earts

"Come live with me and be my love," pleads a love-struck narrator in Christopher Marlowe's poem "The Passionate Shepherd to His Love." The shepherd promises his lover a bed of roses, fragrant posies, and a cap of flowers—all the trappings of a pastoral setting alive with romantic symbols of love, life, and growth.

These new Hearts stamps capture a similar sense of promise and hope. Nancy Stahl—whose previous stamp designs include the New York Public Library Lion, the Art Deco Eagle, and the Snowy Egret—created this artwork after observing a wide range of objects with intertwined designs, such as silver charms or old-fashioned garden gates, adding evocative touches to the timeless symbolism of hearts.

As practical as they are attractive, these stamps are available in two denominations to cover both the one-ounce and the two-ounce mailing rates. Each one-ounce stamp is intended for use on the RSVP envelope often enclosed with a wedding invitation. The two-ounce stamp will accommodate the heavier weight of a wedding invitation with enclosures.

As wedding guests discover these elegant stamps on their invitations, they will attach their own meanings to these designs, seeing in them a gift of precious jewelry or the endless renewal of nature. These stamps will tell them that someone, much like Marlowe's shepherd, has asked a timeless question; and that another, his lover, has happily answered "yes."

and be my love

Pacific Lighthouses

Built to help vessels navigate safely through perilous waters, lighthouses are also landmarks, historical structures, and a beloved subject for American stamps. This new issuance, featuring paintings by longtime lighthouse stamp artist Howard Koslow, again honors the role of these sentinels in safeguarding the nation's maritime interests.

Currently home to the 14th Coast Guard District Commander, Diamond Head Lighthouse is the last occupied light station in Hawaii. First lit in 1899, the tower was replaced with a concrete lighthouse in 1917. Its light warns ships away from the coral reefs south of Oahu and leads them safely into the Honolulu harbor.

Five Finger Lighthouse stands on a small island south of Juneau at the entrance to Alaska's scenic Frederick Sound and Stephens Passage. Fire destroyed the original 1902 wood tower, but it was replaced by a concrete, Art Deco–style tower with a black lantern.

At 107 feet, Grays Harbor Lighthouse—also known as Westport Lighthouse—is the tallest lighthouse in Washington and one of the tallest on the Pacific Coast. Dedicated in 1898, this octagonal tower marks the harbor entrance with distinctive red and white beams.

Located south of Reedsport, Oregon, Umpqua River Lighthouse was the first tower of its kind built in the Oregon Territory. The original was built in 1857, but erosion caused it to collapse, and a new tower was built on higher ground. Visible from a distance of 21 miles, its light flashes two white beams and one red.

Standing on an exposed rock off the coast of northern California, St. George Reef Lighthouse began warning vessels away from danger in 1892. Because continued exposure to the elements made maintenance expensive and duty perilous, this sentinel was deactivated in 1975. It is now on the National Register of Historic Places.

Gerald R. Ford

USA 41

Gerald R. Ford

In 2007, the U.S. Postal Service issued a stamp honoring President Gerald R. Ford, who died on December 26, 2006. President Ford assumed the presidency in 1974 during the gravest constitutional crisis since the Civil War.

Gerald R. Ford was born on July 14, 1913, in Omaha, Nebraska, and was raised in Grand Rapids, Michigan. A graduate of the University of Michigan and Yale Law School, Ford served aboard the USS *Monterey* during World War II. He returned to Grand Rapids, where he married the former Betty Bloomer in October 1948. The Fords had four children, seven grandchildren, and four great-grandchildren.

In November 1948, Ford was elected to the first of 13 terms in the U.S. House of Representatives and quickly established a reputation for personal integrity and political moderation. In 1963, he was appointed to the Warren Commission which investigated the assassination of President John F. Kennedy. By the early 1970s, Ford concluded that he would never realize his ambition to be Speaker of the House and decided to return home in 1977.

But the American people weren't ready to part with Gerald Ford. In December 1973, he was confirmed by Congress as Vice President of the United States—and just eight months later, Ford became America's 38th president. Upon taking the presidential oath, he spoke to the American people: "I am acutely aware that you have not elected me as your President by your ballots, so I ask you to confirm me as your President with your prayers."

More than his many achievements and visionary policy initiatives, the Ford Presidency was defined by his integrity and unbending adherence to the truth. His time in office was also a time of national healing. He announced clemency terms for Vietnam-era draft evaders and pardoned his predecessor in an act that was as personally courageous as it was politically detrimental. In 2001, he received the Profile in Courage Award in tribute to his determination, in issuing the pardon, to place the nation's best interests over his own political future.

Ford remained active in public, civic, and charitable activities. He received the Presidential Medal of Freedom, and he and Mrs. Ford were awarded the Congressional Gold Medal. With the passage of time, the presidency of Gerald Ford is understood with clarity and appreciation. As columnist David Broder summarized even in the final days of Ford's tenure: "In an odd, inexplicable way, the truth has begun to dawn on people . . . that he was the kind of President Americans wanted—and didn't know they had."

FACING PAGE: President Ford at the White House on January 22, 1975. ABOVE LEFT: A contemplative Commander in Chief.
ABOVE RIGHT: A touching moment between President and Mrs. Ford as they watch election returns on November 2, 1976.

MARVEL SUPER HEROES

For decades, Super Heroes have been synonymous with the comic book medium. Their adventures provide an escape from the everyday and demonstrate that individuals can indeed make a difference. The Marvel Super Heroes stamps include 10 character portraits along with reproductions of the artwork from 10 classic comic book covers. Taken together, the stamps on this sheet present a compelling overview of the Marvel artistic vision.

First introduced in 1939 in *Marvel Comics* #1, the Sub-Mariner was one of the earliest stars in the Marvel—then called Timely Comics—universe. The cover art represents a fairly late reincarnation of the character as drawn by two longtime contributors to the Marvel creative team, Sol Brodsky and John Buscema. Gene Colan, who had also been part of the original Timely crew, created the character portrait of this underwater monarch. Colan's work is also featured on the *Invincible Iron Man* #1 cover.

Captain America followed Sub-Mariner in 1941. Created by Joe Simon and Jack Kirby, Captain America profited from the prevailing patriotic sentiment during World War II and became an instant success. The classic cover art shown on the stamp marks the first time since World War II that Captain America starred in his own comic book. Jack Kirby did the cover art; the character portrait is by John Romita.

By 1959, Jack Kirby was working almost exclusively for the Marvel Comics Group. His work can be seen on several of the classic covers from the 1960s: *The Amazing Spider-Man* #1 with Steve Ditko, *The Incredible Hulk* #1, *The X-Men* #1, and *The Fantastic Four* #3. Kirby also created the artwork for the character portraits of the Thing and the Silver Surfer shown on these stamps. He and editor/writer Stan Lee set the tone for many Marvel comic books.

In fact, Stan Lee had created a whole new system of producing the Marvel comics. Instead of beginning with a full script, he began with an idea that could be discussed with the artists. But working with Kirby was different. "Some artists, of course, need a more detailed plot than others," Lee said. "Some artists, such as Jack Kirby, need no plot at all. I mean, I'll just say to Jack, 'Let's let the next villain be Dr. Doom'. . . or I may not even say that. He may tell me."

In 1961, the Fantastic Four, a team created with
Kirby's solid visuals and Lee's flashy dialogue, made its debut.
Lee's distinctive new creations were given recognizable foibles and
squabbled with one another, causing a sensation. Continuing this trend,
the characters in the next generation of Marvel Super Heroes—Spider-Man,
Iron Man, and The Incredible Hulk among them—were plagued by problems
that made it easier for readers to relate.

Until *The Amazing Spider-Man* series debuted in 1963, teenagers in comics had been relegated to the role of sidekicks. The classic cover reproduced
on the stamp is from Spidey's 1963 debut issue, in which Peter worries about
money—an unusual concern for a Super Hero. The character art by John Romita
shows Spider-Man as he looked in 1991.

Iron Man is a modern-day knight prepared to fight any injustice. The cover art by Gene
Colan shows Iron Man captured by villains bent on world domination. The Hulk, another
Lee/Kirby invention, allows creators and fans alike to explore the darker
side of Dr. Bruce Banner, a mild-mannered scientist.

Stan Lee and Jack Kirby also created Marvel's ever-evolving X-Men
series. The 1963 cover art shown on the stamp presents the original five
teenage X-Men characters: Cyclops, Angel, Beast, Iceman, and Marvel
Girl. Wolverine joined the X-Men in 1975, quickly becoming a popular
but brooding anti-hero.

In 1977, Marvel introduced Jessica Drew on the cover of *Marvel
Spotlight* #32. The cover art is the work of artist Gil Kane, considered a
master of the form. The character art by Carmine Infantino shows a close-
up of the later, more developed Spider-Woman character.

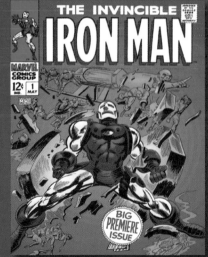

The Daredevil cover art, one of the more recent covers
featured on the stamp pane, showcases the work of Frank
Miller. Credited with transforming the Daredevil
series, Miller focused on the martial arts and
the hero's home turf, Hell's Kitchen in New York City. The
character artwork, also by Frank Miller, celebrates Daredevil's one-time love interest, Elektra, who made her debut
in 1981.

As these stamps amply demonstrate, comic books
aren't simply "kid stuff." Serious artists and writers alike
have contributed to this uniquely American art form.

39

Vintage Mahogany Speedboats

There is something typically American about vintage mahogany speedboats. Both practical and luxurious, they combine time-honored craftsmanship with all the technological advances of the early 20th century. "They go like the wind, yet are easily controlled by boy or girl," reads a typical speedboat advertisement from the 1930s. "They start, stop, steer, turn and reverse like an automobile, yet they are infinitely more flexible."

Each summer the Concours d'Elegance draws recreational boating enthusiasts from around the U.S. and the world to the serene waters of Lake Tahoe. Knowing that such details as leather seats, Art Deco–style trim, and polished planking articulate the beauty and elegance of these classic craft, art director Carl T. Herrman attended the Concours, where he was treated to the sight of more than 100 antique powerboats, all beautifully restored and ready to go at a moment's notice.

Overwhelmed by the number of magnificent speedboats on display, he worked closely with Jim Wanguard of *Classic Boating* magazine and Rebecca Hopfinger, Director of Development and Curator of Special Exhibits at the Antique Boat Museum in Clayton, New York, to identify four essential boats to include on the pane. Renowned boating expert Anthony S. Mollica, Jr., provided additional research assistance.

The boats shown on these stamps reflect the development of wooden speedboats in the United States during the early 20th century. Taken together, they prove that then, as now, the American talent for combining ease with speed is unmatched. Constructed in 1915, the Hutchinson Brothers launch is capable of reaching speeds close to 30 miles per hour. The Gar Wood and Chris-Craft runabouts—built in 1931 and 1936 respectively—can each travel more than 40 miles per hour, and *Thunderbird* was designed in 1939 to be the fastest boat on Lake Tahoe.

Yet to those who know them best, vintage mahogany boats represent more than just speed. "Speedboats are icons of American culture," agrees Herrman. "They are pieces of art, like sculpture."

Louis Comfort Tiffany

Since the debut of the Amish Quilts stamps in 2001, the American Treasures series has been devoted to showcasing beautiful works of American fine arts and crafts. Subsequent issuances have featured artwork by John James Audubon, Mary Cassatt, and Martin Johnson Heade. Recently the series returned to the theme of textiles with stamps depicting New Mexico Rio Grande Blankets and the Quilts of Gee's Bend.

For this year's issuance, art director Derry Noyes opted for a different approach, choosing a leaded Favrile-glass window from the collection of the Metropolitan Museum of Art in New York. Entitled *Magnolias and Irises* and dating to around 1908, this lovely memorial window was designed by Louis Comfort Tiffany (1848–1933) for a mausoleum in a Brooklyn cemetery and later given to the Met by an anonymous donor in 1981.

An opalescent type of stained glass, Favrile glass was named and patented by Tiffany himself; his mastery of the medium is evident in the beautiful variety of colors and textures used to create this lovely stained-glass scene. Magnolia trees and irises bloom on the shore of a lake, while a river wends its way to the lake through overlapping mountains that recede into the background under a cloud-dappled sky. Tiffany often used many of these same elements in his designs for other memorial windows. The winding river, for instance, is appropriately symbolic of the passage of life.

As a young man, Tiffany traveled to Egypt and North Africa, where his eyes were forever opened to a wider range of artistic possibilities. "I returned to New York," he later wrote, "wondering why we made so little use of our eyes, why we refrained so obstinately from taking advantage of color in our architecture and our clothing when Nature indicates its mastership." The window depicted on this stamp demonstrates one of the many ways in which Tiffany used his artist's eye to enrich the visual life of our country, ensuring that his works will always be remembered as true American treasures.

ABOVE RIGHT: *Feeding the Flamingos*, a window designed by Tiffany. RIGHT: Tiffany's Cobweb library lamp, made circa 1900. FACING PAGE: *View of Oyster Bay*, made in 1908 for the William C. Skinner House.

LOUIS COMFORT TIFFANY

Celebrate!

"**Let all thy joys** be as the month of May," implored 17th-century poet Francis Quarles, "and all thy days be as a marriage day." Throughout history, well-wishes have come in many forms, including scrolls, packages, and sealed letters—and sometimes, quite memorably, as poetry.

In fact, since ancient times, poets have composed "occasional" poems, verse written specifically to celebrate special events. Classical poets were especially fond of occasional genres. A *prothalamion*, for example, is a poem that commemorates the wedding day itself, while an *epithalamion* praises the bride and bridegroom. An *encomium*, from the Greek word meaning "revel" or "celebration," enthusiastically praises its honoree, while a *panegyric* pays similar tribute to its subject but is meant to be read in public on a festive occasion.

Whether your celebratory message is a prothalamion or a panegyric, a friendly letter or a simple birthday note, this new stamp hints at the positive sentiment contained within. The recipient will be pleased to see it—for, as W.H. Auden noted in his own panegyric to the postman:

> *And none will hear the postman's knock*
> *Without a quickening of the heart.*
> *For who can bear to feel himself forgotten?*

James Stewart

No one who has seen James Stewart's Oscar-nominated performance in the 1939 classic *Mr. Smith Goes to Washington* is likely to forget it. As the Postal Service set out to honor this great actor, the design team felt that Stewart's work in the role of Jefferson Smith suggested some of the qualities most important about the actor himself: integrity, willingness to work hard, and commitment to his country.

During preliminary design discussions, it quickly became clear that each of Stewart's films had different but equally devout fans. The sheer number of choices revealed something about Stewart's abilities as an actor: in more than 80 movies, whether he was playing the philosophizing Elwood P. Dowd in *Harvey* or George Bailey in *It's a Wonderful Life,* he always seemed to be playing himself.

After Stewart made his film debut in 1934, initial uncertainty about what kinds of roles he should play gave way to the recognition of his star potential. He won his first Oscar nomination for Best Actor in the title role of *Mr. Smith Goes to Washington* and followed that success with his performance in *The Philadelphia Story,* for which he won another Best Actor nomination—and the Oscar as well.

During World War II, Stewart served in the United States Army Air Force, winning multiple decorations. His first movie after the war was the sentimental holiday favorite *It's a Wonderful Life,* after which he appeared in a series of films directed by Alfred Hitchcock. In *Rope,* he played a teacher who solves a murder mystery; in *Rear Window,* he gave a *tour de force* performance as a photographer confined to a wheelchair; in *The Man Who Knew Too Much,* he played a doctor drawn into a sinister web; and in *Vertigo,* often cited as Hitchcock's greatest masterpiece, he played a man obsessed with a mysterious woman. Demonstrating his versatility, during the 1950s and 1960s Stewart also appeared in Westerns, most notably *The Man Who Shot Liberty Valance, Shenandoah,* and *Cheyenne Autumn.*

Throughout his life, Jimmy Stewart and his wife, Gloria, were strong supporters of numerous charitable causes, especially wildlife conservation. Among his many honors were an Oscar for lifetime achievement, awarded in 1985. That same year, he was presented with the Presidential Medal of Freedom—and in 1997, the year he died, Princeton University honored him by dedicating a film theater in his name.

FACING PAGE: Stewart portrayed the whimsical Elwood P. Dowd in the 1950 film *Harvey*. LEFT: Stewart won his first Oscar nomination for his performance in *Mr. Smith Goes to Washington*. TOP: A dignified Stewart in 1971.

Jury Duty

To highlight the role of the jury in the American justice system, stamp artist Lance Hidy focused on the human element: the twelve jurors who deliberate about the guilt or innocence of their peers. Hidy, who previously designed stamps to honor mentoring programs and the Special Olympics, decided to show the silhouetted profiles of twelve jurors of various colors and creeds. He wanted to emphasize that jury duty is a privilege—and that citizens should serve with pride.

The purpose of a trial by one's peers is twofold: it protects the accused from unfounded criminal charges and from the biases of persons who might be too easily influenced. The right to a trial by jury was included in the constitutions of all thirteen original states and was eventually enshrined in U.S. law. Later amendments to the Constitution extended the privilege of jury service to women and African-American citizens.

The current American jury system is based on legal procedures established in medieval England during the rule of King Henry II. At that time, "assizes" brought twelve local men together to resolve questions over ownership and inheritance. In 1215, King John signed the Magna Carta, subjecting the monarch to the rule of law. According to the Magna Carta, "no free man shall be seized or imprisoned . . . except by the lawful judgment of his peers or by the law of the land."

In England and in the American colonies, juries appeared reluctant to convict the accused in less serious cases, due to the customary penalty of death. Thus, juries acquired the reputation of being protectors of individual liberty. In the colonies, the British retaliated against American juries by setting up special courts in which jury trials were not used. The citizenry of the colonies felt so strongly about this infringement of their rights that they included it as one of their complaints in the Declaration of Independence: the British king had deprived them of the "benefits of trial by jury."

Today, jury service remains a cornerstone of American democracy. The diverse group of twelve citizens shown in the stamp art represents the diversity of the American population and underscores the need for all to participate—the best way to guarantee citizens a trial by their peers.

JURY DUTY

SERVE WITH PRIDE
USA 41

Alpine Tundra

Beginning above
the tree line in high mountain areas such as the Rockies, the treeless region of the alpine tundra has a climate much like that of the arctic tundra—but the reason for the similarity has little to do with proximity to the North Pole. Instead, the cold, snowy winters of the alpine tundra are due to high elevation, where temperatures are lower, winds are fierce, and solar radiation is intensified by the thinner atmosphere.

Featuring a painting by series artist John D. Dawson, the ninth Nature of America pane highlights a fascinating ecosystem where wildlife must cope with harsh conditions—and where survival depends on making the most of the short alpine summer. Animals have just three or four months to breed and prepare for the coming winter by building up body fat and storing food in dens and burrows. As winter approaches, most of them seek more hospitable conditions at lower elevations or migrate to warmer climes. Only the hardiest species remain, relying on adaptations such as thick coats; furry paws or feathered feet and legs; white fur or feathers that serve as protective camouflage; and, in some cases, the ability to hibernate.

Tundra plants are well adapted to the climate. All of them are frost resistant; most grow close to the ground and have extensive root systems that anchor them against the wind, collect water, and store nutrients. Some have hair-like growths or waxy coatings that protect them from the elements, and some have red pigment or other colors that help convert light rays to heat. The buds on many flowering plants mature under the snows of winter and spring, bursting into bloom almost as soon as summer arrives.

This stamp pane depicts a summer tundra scene about 12,000 feet up in Rocky Mountain National Park in northern Colorado. Snow still lingers on the highest slopes and in a few sheltered basins; large mammals graze in the open, while smaller mammals stay close to the rocks, ready to take cover if threatened by a predator. Meanwhile, birds and butterflies take flight or feed among colorful flowers. With this vivid depiction of a vital American ecosystem, the Postal Service continues to promote the appreciation of major plant and animal communities—especially those that amaze us with their hardiness in the harshest of nature's climes.

Mendez *v.* Westminster School District

The story of *Mendez et al v. Westminster School District of Orange County et al*, a groundbreaking legal case, begins in 1944, when immigrants Gonzalo and Felicitas Mendez were building a life in Westminster, a small farming community south of Los Angeles. The newly opened elementary school refused to admit their children; instead, the Mendez children were expected to attend one of many specially designated "Mexican schools" common at that time in California and throughout the Southwest. After Gonzalo Mendez discussed the situation with school officials, the school board offered his children "special admission." Deciding instead to stand up for the rights of all children, he joined with other Latino parents to sue four school districts—Westminster, Santa Ana, Garden Grove, and El Modena—on behalf of some 5,000 students.

The plaintiffs' attorney, David Marcus, successfully attacked the "separate but equal" doctrine. On February 18, 1946, Federal District Judge Paul J. McCormick ruled that merely providing the same textbooks, courses, and comparable facilities in separate schools does not give students equal protection under the law and that social equality is a "paramount requisite" in America's public school system.

On June 14, 1947, California governor Earl Warren signed a bill outlawing segregated schools. In 1953, Warren was appointed Chief Justice of the United States; the following year, the Supreme Court issued its landmark ruling in *Brown v. Board of Education* declaring segregation illegal nationwide.

The *Mendez* ruling that school districts could not segregate on the basis of national origin thus established an important legal precedent. The parents who joined with Gonzalo and Felicitas Mendez in the fight for their children deserve a place of honor in the American story.

The Art of Disney:
MAGIC

"**The world** is full of magical things patiently waiting for our wits to grow sharper," a wise philosopher once wrote. With these new stamps in the Art of Disney series, the U.S. Postal Service explores the idea of magic as envisioned by Walt Disney and his studio animators—and as portrayed by a cast of magical Disney favorites.

In the classic story of Dumbo, an innocent little elephant turns his oversized ears into an even larger triumph, imparting a very big truth: It's not the "magic feather" that helps you soar, but the magic of believing in yourself.

Anyone who's ever dreamed of flying with Peter Pan and Tinker Bell knows that all it takes is faith, trust, and pixie dust. Whatever our age, these magical characters will always lead us to Never Land, where we and our dreams remain forever young.

As Mickey Mouse—depicted on this stamp as "The Sorcerer's Apprentice"—gleefully wields his newfound powers, we share his exuberance. What could be better than commanding the galaxies? Things soon get out of control, but the spunky little fellow still shows us the magic in reaching for your dreams.

Just when Aladdin needs help the most, he discovers a battered lamp that reveals a wisecracking, wish-granting genie. Genie can work many wonders, but his actions prove that sometimes a true-blue friend is all the magic we need.

Designed by David Pacheco and illustrated by Peter Emmerich, these delightful stamps remind us that Disney magic is more than mere fantasy. Its deeper meaning lies in the wonder, laughter, and hope that these characters and stories bring to our lives as they help us discover the magic of our own imaginations.

Polar Lights

In "The Ballad of the Northern Lights," poet Robert Service vividly describes the aurora borealis: "It swept the sky like a giant scythe," his narrator exclaims, recounting how he beheld with "wild, uplifted eyes" the sight of fiery pennants and weaving streams "in the battlefield of the skies." Visitors to the polar regions react with similar awe, and even scientists ponder the humbling beauty of the wintry heavens as they work to gain a better understanding of this magnificent phenomenon.

Visible in both polar regions, the polar lights are the result of a magnetic storm, when Earth's magnetic field is unusually active due to a dynamic interaction with the sun. Energetic electrons descend from space and collide with molecules in the upper atmosphere, leading to the emission of green and sometimes red light. The lights come in different visual forms, including arcs, curtains, and rays, and are a relatively common sight in Alaska, Canada, and northern Europe. During particularly intense magnetic storms, polar lights can occasionally be seen in some of the lower 48 states as well.

Folklore and legend have long played a role in how humans have viewed the polar lights. The very names of this phenomenon—aurora borealis in the northern hemisphere and aurora australis in the south—evoke the mythological Aurora, the ancient Roman goddess of the dawn. The rosy-cheeked deity was thought to wear robes of dazzling colors and ride through the air on a brightly colored chariot drawn by white horses.

In some parts of Scandinavia, the lights were believed to be heavenly reflections of large swarms of herring or the emanations of watchful—and sometimes vengeful—spirits. By contrast, the Inuit people of Siberia and North America are said to have developed a more whimsical explanation, believing that the lights emanated from the spirits of the dead as they played games with a walrus skull in the sky.

Today, specialists who investigate the polar lights understand that the beautiful sight is the result of a magnetic storm. But often, even scientists are amazed by the marvelous sight of luminous arcs and curtains in the sky—a reaction that gives them a true point of kinship with their clever and curious ancestors.

USA 41

Aurora Australis

HOLIDAY KNITS

In recent years, knitting has become quite popular again, not only in the United States but also internationally. In 2007, just in time for the start of the winter holiday season, the Postal Service joined in the fun by issuing four stamps that feature classic Christmastime imagery as envisioned by nationally known illustrator Nancy Stahl.

Inspired by traditional Norwegian sweaters and knitted Christmas stockings, Stahl decided to focus on "something cozy." She used computer software to draw her original designs and convert them to stitches and rows; then she downloaded the information to an electronic knitting machine and used it to knit her creations. Unfortunately, that machine's smaller stitch gauge didn't provide the effect that she was hoping to achieve.

To perfect a project which she increasingly considered a "labor of love," Stahl transferred the same designs onto punch cards and used a different knitting machine that had a larger stitch gauge and worked something like an old Jacquard loom. She scanned the finished pieces into her computer, retouching the photographic images to ensure that all the stitches aligned properly.

The resulting stamps—a dignified stag, a snow-dappled evergreen tree, a perky snowman, and a whimsical teddy bear—combined to form a colorful and indeed cozy issuance; each stamp will surely add an extra touch of warmth to seasonal correspondence.

The Madonna of the Carnation
by Bernardino Luini

Since 1978, the theme of each Christmas stamp has been the Madonna and Child, a subject that has attracted a devoted following. This year's Christmas issuance features *The Madonna of the Carnation*, an oil-on-panel painting by Bernardino Luini. Dating to around 1515, the painting is now part of the Samuel H. Kress Collection at the National Gallery of Art in Washington, DC.

Few details are known about Luini's life, but his artistic legacy ensures his place in history as one of the world's master painters. He was a prominent member of Northern Italy's Lombard School, which was centered in Milan. Powerfully influenced by Leonardo da Vinci, Lombard artists generally executed their drawings and paintings from life, imbuing the best of their works—whether portraits, still lifes, or devotional paintings—with an immediacy that continues to transcend the centuries.

Born in the small town of Luino on the shores of Lake Maggiore, Bernardino Luini was already a distinguished painter when he moved, sometime around 1500, to Milan. A popular artist during his own lifetime, Luini operated a busy and successful workshop where he trained numerous apprentices and accepted commissions not only in Milan but also in nearby towns. Many of his frescoes and altarpieces can still be seen in Lombard churches, and his easel paintings now reside in museums around the world.

In painting *The Madonna of the Carnation*, Luini used oil paints—then a relatively new medium—to great advantage. He enhanced his typically warm palette with the technique known as *sfumato*, an Italian word meaning "smoky," in which softened color gradations and blended tones create the illusion of depth, volume, and contour. Positioned against a plain, dark background and bathed in glowing light, Luini's sacred figures seem alive and humanly accessible, filling the picture plane and inviting the viewer's undivided attention.

During the Middle Ages and the Renaissance, carnations were symbolic of both the crucifixion and the Virgin's pure love. The pensive expressions on the faces of Luini's exquisitely modeled figures would have conveyed to Renaissance viewers the Virgin's foreknowledge and Christ's acceptance of his future death on the cross. By featuring this stunning work of art, this stamp evokes a sense of faith and family that will endure throughout the Christmas season.

FACING PAGE: *Saint Mary and Child*, a work by Luini from around 1510. RIGHT: *Madonna and Child in Glory*, an early 16th-century work by Antonio Allegri Correggio.

Photo Credits

COVER

© Peter Kun Frary, Honolulu, Hawaii

TITLE PAGE

© Ann Cecil/www.anncecil.com

BLACK HERITAGE: ELLA FITZGERALD

Page 10: © Underwood & Underwood/ CORBIS

Pages 10–11: © Herman Leonard/Redferns Music Picture Library

Pages 12–13: (photograph and album covers) Ella Fitzgerald Collection, Archives Center, National Museum of American History, Behring Center, Smithsonian Institution

Pages 13: (lower right) Art courtesy Photofest.

OKLAHOMA STATEHOOD

Page 14: © Richard Cummins/CORBIS

Page 15: © Richard Cummins/CORBIS

Pages 14–15: (background) © Danny Lehman/CORBIS

WITH LOVE AND KISSES

HERSHEY'S, KISSES, the plume and the product configuration are registered trademarks used with permission from the Hershey Company.

Pages 16–17: Archival images courtesy of Hershey Community Archives, Hershey, PA

LITERARY ARTS: HENRY WADSWORTH LONGFELLOW

Pages 18–19: Wood, Grant (1892-1942) The Midnight Ride of Paul Revere. 1931. Oil on masonite, H. 30, W. 40 in. (76.2 x 101.6 cm). Arthur Hoppock Hearn Fund, 1950 (50.117). Image © The Metropolitan Museum of Art/ Source: Art Resource, NY

Page 19: (portrait) Courtesy National Park Service, Longfellow National Historic Site

SETTLEMENT OF JAMESTOWN

Page 20: (upper right) Courtesy APVA Preservation Virginia/Historic Jamestowne

Pages 20–21: (background) © Bettmann/ CORBIS

Page 22: Art by Richard Schlecht © 2006 U.S. Postal Service

Page 23: (top and bottom) © Richard T. Nowitz/CORBIS

STAR WARS

© 2007 Lucasfilm Ltd. & TM. All rights reserved. Used under authorization.

Pages 24–25: (star field in background) © Digital Art/CORBIS

Pages 26–27: (star field in background) © Roger Ressmeyer/CORBIS

POLLINATION

Pages 28–29: © Gray Hardel/CORBIS

HEARTS

Page 30: The Art Archive/Theatre Museum London/Graham Brandon

Page 31: © Ariel Skelley/Blend Images/ CORBIS

PACIFIC LIGHTHOUSES

Pages 32–33: Michael Wood/Acclaim Images

Page 33: (lower left) © Stephen M. Corley/ www.nicelights.com

GERALD R. FORD

Page 34: Arnold Newman/Getty Images

Page 35: (top) © CORBIS; (bottom) Courtesy Gerald R. Ford Library

MARVEL SUPER HEROES

Pages 36–39: Name(s) of character(s) and the distinctive likeness(es) thereof are Trademarks of Marvel Characters, Inc. and are used with permission. © 2007 Marvel Characters, Inc. All Rights Reserved. Super Heroes is a co-owned registered trademark.

Acknowledgments

These stamps and this stamp-collecting book were produced by Stamp Services, Government Relations, United States Postal Service.

JOHN E. POTTER
Postmaster General, Chief Executive Officer

DAVID E. FAILOR
Executive Director, Stamp Services

THOMAS G. DAY
Senior Vice President, Government Relations

Special thanks are extended to the following individuals for their contributions to the production of this book:

UNITED STATES POSTAL SERVICE

TERRENCE W. McCAFFREY
Manager, Stamp Development

CINDY L. TACKETT
Manager, Stamp Products and Exhibitions

SONJA D. EDISON
Project Manager

HARPERCOLLINS PUBLISHERS

PHIL FRIEDMAN
Publisher, Collins Reference

LUCY ALBANESE
Design Director, General Books Group

SUSAN KOSKO
Production Director, General Books Group

MARINA PADAKIS
Senior Production Editor

NIGHT & DAY DESIGN

TIMOTHY SHANER
Art Director, Designer

PHOTOASSIST, INC.

MARY STEPHANOS
JEFF SYPECK
GREG VARNER
Editorial Consultants

MICHAEL OWENS
Photo Editor

KATE GRIFFIN
REBECCA HIRSH
JENNY TRUCANO
CRISTEN WILLS
Photo Research

SARAH HANDWERGER
MICHAEL OWENS
Rights and Permissions

JENNY TRUCANO
CRISTEN WILLS
Traffic Coordinators

THE CITIZENS' STAMP ADVISORY COMMITTEE

BENJAMIN F. BAILAR
CARY R. BRICK
MICHAEL R. BROCK
DONNA DE VARONA
DAVID L. ENYON
JEAN PICKER FIRSTENBERG
DR. HENRY LOUIS GATES, JR.
SYLVIA HARRIS
JESSICA HELFAND
I. MICHAEL HEYMAN
JOHN M. HOTCHNER
KARL MALDEN
JAMES N. MIHO
JOAN A. MONDALE
B. MARTIN PEDERSEN
RONALD A. ROBINSON

Photo Credits

VINTAGE MAHOGANY SPEEDBOATS
Page 40: © Neil Rabinowitz/CORBIS
Page 41: (top) © The Mariner's Museum/
CORBIS; (bottom) © ROB &SAS/CORBIS

**AMERICAN TREASURES:
LOUIS COMFORT TIFFANY**
The leaded Favrile-glass window titled
Magnolias and Irises that is featured on
the stamp is courtesy The Metropolitan
Museum of Art, Anonymous Gift, in
memory of Mr. and Mrs. A.B. Frank,
1981 (1981.159) Photograph © 1981
The Metropolitan Museum of Art.
Page 42: (portrait) Photograph of Louis
Comfort Tiffany. The Charles Hosmer
Morse Museum of American Art, Winter
Park, FL. © The Charles Hosmer Morse
Foundation, Inc.; (lamp photograph)
Library lamp, c.1900. Cobweb design,
No. 146. Leaded glass, mosaic, bronze.
Tiffany Studios. 62-020. The Charles
Hosmer Morse Museum of American Art,
Winter Park, FL. © The Charles Hosmer
Morse Foundation, Inc.
Page 43: View of Oyster Bay, c.1908.
William C. Skinner House, New York.
Leaded glass. Tiffany Studios. 69-001.
The Charles Hosmer Morse Museum of
American Art, Winter Park, FL. © The
Charles Hosmer Morse Foundation, Inc.
Image © The Metropolitan Museum of
Art, lent by the Charles Hosmer Morse
Museum of American Art, Winter Park,
Florida, in memory of Charles Hosmer
Morse (L.1978.19)

CELEBRATE!
Pages 44–45: © Royalty-Free/CORBIS

**LEGENDS OF HOLLYWOOD:
JAMES STEWART**
Page 46: "Harvey" and "Vertigo," courtesy
of Universal Studios Licensing LLLP,
Art courtesy Photofest. CHEYENNE
AUTUMN © Warner Bros. Inc. All
Rights Reserved. Art courtesy Photofest.
THE SHOP AROUND THE CORNER
© Turner Entertainment Co. A Warner

Bros. Entertainment Company. All Rights
Reserved. Art Courtesy Photofest.
Page 47: (top right) © Barnabas Bosshart/
CORBIS; (bottom left): "MR. SMITH
GOES TO WASHINGTON" © 1939,
renewed 1967 Columbia Pictures
Industries, Inc. All Rights Reserved.
Courtesy of Columbia Pictures. Art
courtesy Photofest.

JURY DUTY
Page 48: (background) © Lew Long/CORBIS.
(bottom) © Royalty-Free/CORBIS
Page 49: © Royalty-Free/CORBIS

**NATURE OF AMERICA:
ALPINE TUNDRA**
Pages 50–51: (background) © David
Muench/CORBIS
Page 51: (top) © Chase Swift/CORBIS.
(center) © W. Perry Conway/CORBIS.
(bottom) © John Conrad/CORBIS

**MENDEZ V. WESTMINSTER
SCHOOL DISTRICT**
Pages 52–53: © Royalty-Free/CORBIS

THE ART OF DISNEY: MAGIC
Disney Materials © Disney
Pages 54–55: Art by Peter Emmerich.

POLAR LIGHTS
Pages 56–57: (background) © Steve Voss/
www.astrokiwi.com; (top) © LeRoy
Zimmerman/www.photosymphony.com

HOLIDAY KNITS
Page 58: Art by Nancy Stahl © 2006 U.S.
Postal Service
Page 59: (lower left) © Ariel Skelley/CORBIS

**THE MADONNA OF THE CARNATION
BY BERNARDINO LUINI**
Madonna of the Carnation, Bernardino
Luini, National Gallery of Art,
Washington, D.C.
Page 60: (background) Erich Lessing/Art
Resource, NY.
Page 61: © Summerfield Press/CORBIS